BECO

Hypnotic Influence Ninja

Published by Transform Destiny, Inc
17332 Irvine Blvd Ste 235
Tustin CA 92780 USA

www.HypnoticNinja.com

ISBN-10: 097445995X
ISBN-13: 978-0-9744599-5-0

Printed in the United States of America
10 9 8 7 6 5 4 3 2

FOREWORD

From One Ninja to Another

You're about to embark on a journey down the rabbit hole of the inner-mind. In this book, you'll learn principles that people (including myself) have paid thousands of dollars for, to learn to influence and persuade people hypnotically in your personal and professional life.

These principles are so powerful, people in marketing, business, military and government everywhere are clammoring to get this knowledge. They are so powerful, they were even used to win the Presidential office in the United States in 2008. Practice these principles with good intentions and integrity, grasshopper

If you'd like to learn more about *traditional* hypnosis, please visit www.learnhypnosisnow.com and get my book, *Learn Hypnosis... Now!*, or my home study course, *Learn Hypnosis... At Home!,* or my *Covert Conversational Hypnosis Home Study Course.*

I hope you enjoy this book, and if you have any questions or comments, please contact me at www.TransformDestiny. com.

-Michael Stevenson

PART ONE

Ten Ways to Become More Hypnotic Now

INTRODUCTION

BECOMING A
Hypnotic Influence Ninja

The average person thinks that hypnosis is some spooky, mystical voodoo where the hypnotist waves a shiny object and the subject becomes a slobbering zombie.

Nothing could be further from the truth. Hypnosis is the induction of "trance," which is often associated with deep relaxation and drool, but often happens in everyday conversation.

If I could redefine trance in a more meaningful way it would be this:

Trance (trăns) v. Moving a person from one state of mind to another.

Taking that definition, we're always in trance. We go through the day, moving from this trance to that trance, all the time.

If you want to influence people, you just need to think of what trance they need to be in and then move them to it.

If you want to sell a prospect something, they need to be moved from their "not interested," trance, to a "buying" trance.

If you want to borrow something from a friend, you need to move them from their "I'm busy right now," trance into a "doing favors" trance.

If you want to get your partner in the mood, you need to move them from their "I just want to watch TV," trance, into a "sexy" trance.

Hypnotic influence is not about getting people to do things against their will. That's actually not possible, no matter how hypnotic you are.

Rather, hypnotic influence is just about moving people from one state of mind — or trance — to another. The greatest communicators, sales pros, negotiators, and yes, even seducers, all know this intuitively.

Within moments of finishing this riveting book, you'll be armed with the tools to hypnotically influence anyone, easily and effortlessly. You'll watch in amazement as resistance melts away. The things you'll hear will blow your mind. And, once you've mastered these tools, you'll feel more confident than, perhaps, ever before. And that will make you a hypnotic influence ninja. So let's get started!

CHAPTER ONE

THE GATEWAY
To The Mind

The key to moving people into trance lies in the subconscious mind – the other part of your mind that is out of your awareness – often called the Unconscious Mind, by hypnotists.

Your Unconscious is the part of you that runs your body, protects you from harm, manages your memories, stores your beliefs and values, runs your habits and generates your emotions.

When it comes to influence, it's important to remember that people don't make decisions logically – they make them emotionally. When President Barrack Obama used hypnotic language patterns to win the Presidential election, he didn't make a logical case for his presidency, like his competitors. He brought people to tears and moved them to vote by tapping into their emotions.

The Unconscious mind does not think in words, like your conscious mind does. It instead thinks in pictures, sounds and feelings.

Think of your last good daydream. As you sit there in your chair, perhaps staring at one spot or another, your eyes defocus, your facial muscles relax, and all the sounds of the day begin to fade away as you lose yourself in the internal world of the Unconscious mind.

As you do this, that chatter that usually exists inside your mind disappears. Your Unconscious mind takes over as the words disappear, and you get lost in the imagination.

To unlock the gateway to the mind and hypnotically influence others, you must learn to tap into this emotional conduit by painting pictures, sounds and feelings that move people.

Sensory language that engages people's imagination and emotions is one of the most powerful hypnotic tools available. It is often said that if you want a person to do something for you, take them there in their mind, first.

When I want to convince someone to come to one of my hypnosis trainings, for example, I use language like the following:

"Bill, when you come to this training and see the material I'm teaching, I know you'll be as excited as I was when I first learned it. You'll connect with people just like you who also have a burning desire to be heard, to give yourself a voice, and to learn to influence others with integrity.

"Imagine hearing yourself speaking to others in a way that's powerful, confident, and influential, and how it makes you feel to see yourself finally achieving all those things you want in life. When you think about it that way, I know you can see all the reasons why this sounds like a great idea, doesn't it?"

Notice how I'm using visual words (see, imagine), auditory words (heard, voice, hearing, sounds), and feeling words (excited, connect, burning, powerful, confident, feel).

These words engage the listener, cause them to "go inside" to create that experience, and, ultimately, move them into a trance of your design.

There is one important thing to point out. Since the Unconscious mind thinks in pictures, sounds and feelings, it has a very hard time processing negatives. Negatives are virtually impossible to represent using pictures, sounds and feelings. You just can't not think about something without thinking about it first.

This is one of the biggest mistakes I hear novice influencers make. They create the wrong trance by using negatives.

Anyone who has ever told a child to "not spill the milk," has seen this play out. When you say, "don't spill your milk," the child has to immediately make a picture of spilling the milk in their mind, just to understand the words. This puts the child into a "clumsy trance," and they reach right out and spill the milk!

If you tell someone not to eat the cookies in the kitchen,

they say, "Cookies?! Where?!" You've moved them into a "hungry trance," just by mentioning them.

Many novice influencers try to begin with statements like these:

"You probably won't want to do this..."

"I'm sure you're not interested..."

"Now, don't be offended..."

"Don't be alarmed..."

"This isn't what you think it is..."

While these statements might seem to be influential to the average influencer, you, being a hypnotic influence ninja, now know negative statements like these will absolutely destroy your chances of influencing people powerfully.

The following examples will give you some hypnotic words and phrases to practice using sensory information.

Visual words: See, look, see, view, appear, show, dawn, reveal, envision, illuminate, imagine, clear, foggy, focused, hazy, crystal, picture, colorful, brilliant, bright, beautiful.

Visual phrases: An eyeful, Appears to me, Beyond a shadow of a doubt, Bird's eye view, Catch a glimpse of,

Clear cut, Dim view, Flashed on   , Get a perspective on, Get a scope on, Hazy Idea, Horse of a different color, In light of , In person, In view of, Looks like, Make a scene, Mental image, Mental picture, Mind's eye, Naked eye, Paint a picture, See to it, Short sighted, Showing off, Sight for sore eyes, Staring off into space, Take a peek, Tunnel vision, Under your nose, Up front

Auditory words: Hear, listen, sound(s), make music, harmonize, tune in/out, be all ears, rings a bell, silence, be heard, resonate, deaf, dissonance, question, unhearing

Auditory phrases: Afterthought, Blabbermouth, Clear as a bell, Clearly expressed, Call on   , Describe in detail, Earful , Give an account of, Give me your ear, Grant an audience, Heard voices, Hidden message, Hold your tongue. Idle talk, Inquire into, Keynote speaker, Loud and clear, Manner of speaking, Pay attention to, Power of speech, Purrs like a kitten, State your purpose, Tattle-tale, To tell the truth, Tongue-tied, Tuned in/tuned out, Unheard of, Utterly, Voiced an opinion, Well informed, Within hearing, Word for word

Feeling words: Feel, touch, grasp, get hold of, slip through, catch on, tap into, make contact, throw out, turn around, hard, unfeeling, concrete, scrape, get a handle, solid.

Feeling phrases: All washed up, Boils down to, Chip off the old block, Come to grips with, Control yourself, Cool/calm/collected, Firm foundations, Get a handle on, Get a load of this, Get in touch with, Get the drift of, Get your goat, Hand in hand, Hang in there, Heated argument, Hold it!, Hold on!, Hothead, Keep your shirt on, Know-how, Lay cards on table, Pain-in the neck, Pull some strings, Sharp as a tack, Slipped my mind, Smooth operator, So-so, Start from scratch, Stiff upper lip, Stuffed shirt, Too much of a hassle, Topsy-turvy

CHAPTER TWO

PACING

And Leading

Wouldn't it be great if you could make someone listen to you? Even the greatest of hypnotists can't force people to do what they don't want to do, but what if you had a way to keep people listening and keep them open and receptive to your ideas, no matter what?

Pacing and leading allows you to begin in the subject's trance, and lead them into yours. Without first pacing, or matching, the subject's trance, you have no hope of leading them into your trance.

Imagine that you're having a great day, and when you get to work, one of your co-workers is really grumpy. What do you think will happen if you wave at them and say, "Hey, it's a FANTASTIC day today, isn't it?!"

Of course, because you're conflicting with their trance, you will lose all of your hypnotic mojo! They will probably sneer at you and avoid you all day long.

If you've ever been in a conversation with someone who disagrees with you, then you know the feeling that comes up when someone mismatches your trance. You get defensive, you dig your proverbial feet in, and communication shuts down and you become determined to prove your point over theirs.

To be a hypnotic influence ninja, you have to learn to lead people into your trance gracefully.

Begin by matching things you notice about your subject. How are they standing or sitting? What is their posture? Is their head tilted or straight. ? Do they have a certain look on their face?

These are all physical characteristics of your subject that can be matched. When two people are in *rapport* — a feeling as if they like each other — studies have shown that their physical movements begin to get into sync.

Because the mind-body is a feedback system, when it sees someone in sync, it begins to create that feeling of rapport, automatically. It's like magic, and it happens completely out of the subject's conscious awareness!

This was the "magical" quality that famed hypnotherapist Milton H. Erickson had that allowed him to ask his clients to do nearly *anything*, and they would.

Next, listen to their tone of voice. Is their throat open or pinched? Is the pitch high or low? Rough or smooth? Loud or quiet? Are they speaking fast or slow?

Match the elements of their voice, but be careful of accents!

The point of matching your subject is to create unconscious rapport, not to catch their conscious attention and make them think you're mimicking them! Rapport is to be done subtly, so as to only tickle the unconscious mind.

Next, begin to listen to the ideas and expressions of the subject. They will be telling you about their trance, and you had better match it, or at least respect it, if you want to have any hypnotic influence.

If you're subject says, "I'm really angry with you right now!" don't say, "No you're not!" or it will make them angrier!

Even if you get defensive and say, "Hey, I didn't do anything wrong!" you're going to mismatch their trance and lose all hope of leading them out of it.

Instead, learn to match or respect their trance. Consider the following response:

"I can see that you're really angry, and you have a right to be! I would be angry to, if I thought someone had done that to me!"

Said with the same physiology, same intensity of voice, and respecting the trance that they're in will immediately begin to diffuse the situation. The best part is, you haven't admitted any wrong-doing or assumed any blame. You've only matched their trance.

Once you've matched it, begin to lead them out of it, subtly, little by little. Her's a further example.

Client: "I'm so pissed off that you screwed my order up, I'm *never* going to do business with you people again!"

Ninja: "You *are* really pissed off, and you have a right to be! I would be angry to, if I thought someone had done that to me! And the first thing I would do is yell and scream at the person. As a matter of fact, I'm pretty pissed off that you were treated this way. I'm going to see what I can do right now to fix this situation for you. If I can do that, you'd be willing to think about keeping your account with us?"

As you can see, this exchange would totally take the wind out of the client's sales. It would be virtually impossible for this client to continue their tirade after pulling out these hypnotic ninja skills.

If you were in a sales situation and your prospect said, "I'm not sold yet," you wouldn't reply with, "What? Not sold?! Of course you are, this is the best product in the field!" That would surely break rapport!

Instead, pace and lead them to the buying trance. "That's right, you're not sold. That's because you haven't asked the one question that will have you totally and completely sold right now. So what's on your mind?"

Pacing and leading is one of the most powerful hypnotic ninja skills in your arsenal and applies to every other principle in this book. Practice it well and you'll become more influential almost immediately.

CHAPTER THREE

CAUSE
And Effect

Hypnotic influence ninjas know that linking their suggestions to other things makes them more powerful. This next principle is a perfect example of that.

Cause and Effect is a way of linking one thing to another. We say things like this all the time:

> "The earthquake caused the picture to fall off the wall."
> "If you stick your finger in a power socket, you'll get shocked."
> "It's cold in here because the door is open."
> "Since you're late, we're going to miss the movie."

In all of these statements, it's pretty clear that one thing causes another.

When we hear Cause and Effect statements like these, as long as the cause is plausible, we tend to accept the effect part of the statement. And this is where Cause and Effect becomes so powerful.

Cause and Effect statements take the following forms:

"X makes you Y."

"If X, then Y."

"Since X, then Y."

"As you X, then you Y."

"Y because X."

Or any other language that assumes one thing caused another.

Here are some examples of using these statements persuasively:

"Reading this page makes you want to devour the rest of the book."

"If you use this one technique, then you'll want to tell all your friends."

"Since you're reading these words, you're becoming a hypnotic ninja."

"As you influence people, you'll want to tell them about me."

"You'll want to buy my products, because Barrack Obama used hypnotic patterns to win the Presidency."

Notice that the Cause and Effect relationship does not have to be true. It only has to sound plausible enough for them to accept the suggestion.

This is one of the most powerful tools in your hypnotic ninja arsenal, and the more you use it, the more you'll want to discover.

CHAPTER FOUR

YES SETS AND
The Hypnotic Nod

You're sitting there, reading this book, absorbing these words, and learning how to become a hypnotic influence ninja, and that means you'll want to learn more from me, doesn't it?

The fact is, we're very repetitive creatures, and when we get into a routine, we tend to follow it. Enter the "Yes Set."

The Yes Set causes a person to agree with you, almost out of sheer repetitiveness. The idea is to say several things in a row, to which the subject will say, "yes."

For example, I opened this tip with several statements. "You're sitting there (yes), reading this book (yes), and learning how to become a hypnotic influence ninja (yes)..." Each of these is undeniable.

I follow-up these yeses with the suggestion I want you to accept: "... and that means, you'll want to learn more from me (yes!)..."

The key to Yes Sets is to make observations that the subject will undeniably say yes to. The moment you mismatch them and say something questionable, your hypnotic influence is lost.

There are two keys to this. First, keep things lacking in detail. The less detail the better. You can sometimes get away with saying things that are so ambiguous they don't really mean anything at all, yet they're still true.

For instance, "There you are, doing what you're doing, and you're doing it for a reason which you may or may not know, and that means..."

The second key is the Hypnotic Nod, one of the subtlest yet most powerful hypnotic influence tools.

As you say each statement in the Yes Set, lock eyes with your subject and begin nodding your head. Start off very subtly, and build it up towards the end into a full head nod. You'll find that your subject will begin nodding with you, even if they don't want to – it's that powerful!

CHAPTER FIVE

HYPNOTIC
Assumptions

Another hypnotic influence skill is the art of hypnotic assumptions, called presuppositions. To presuppose simply means to assume something without really saying it.

One classic presupposition was used in retail sales for years. Most sales people were trained to never ask, "Do you want to buy that?" because the answer might be, "No." Instead, they would walk up as you were holding a product and ask, "Will that be cash or check?"

This more powerful question assumes that you're going to buy the product. It's not a question of yes or no. This causes you to make a picture in your head of buying the product, which you're more likely to do now. Pretty sneaky!

I used a presupposition in the beginning of this book when I said, "Within moments of finishing this riveting book, you'll be armed…" Notice that I didn't say, "If you finish this book," because the word "If" creates doubt. Instead, I *assume* that you will do what I want you to do.

Here's another example. If I wanted you to think this book has got incredibly influential language patterns in it, I wouldn't just say, "This book has incredibly influential language patterns," because you might choose to second-guess or challenge my suggestion. It's too direct.

One way to presuppose it would be like this: "Have you seen the incredibly influential language patterns in this book yet?"

This presupposition takes the critical awareness off the suggestion that the book has "incredibly influential language patterns," and turns the focus on whether or not you've seen them. You have to *assume* the book has these incredibly influential language patterns to answer the question of whether you've seen them. The second presupposition is in the word, "yet," which assumes that you will eventually see them — once you buy it!

Presuppositions are what we call, "positive suggestive language." But the most amazing thing about them is that they don't *have* to be positive!

I could get you to assume the same suggestion by saying, "You haven't seen the incredibly influential language patterns in this book yet." Even though it's a negative statement, you still have to assume and accept the same suggestion! This is sneaky ninja stuff!

Here are some hypnotic influence examples of using presuppositions:

"Joe, you're going to find yourself excited once you get my product into your home." (Assumes the product will

get into his home)

"How many ways do you know that book this has benefitted you?" (Assumes the book has benefitted him, the only question is how many ways)

"Should I pick you up Friday night or Saturday night?" (Assumes you will pick them up)

"There are five reasons you'll want to finish this book and one of them is that you enjoy it so much." (Assumes there are five good reasons, even though you only have to give one — very powerful!)

"When you think of the ways you can afford my product, buying it now is an easy decision, isn't it?" (Assumes the prospect has ways of affording it they may not be thinking of, yet, until you mentioned it)

CHAPTER SIX

INFLUENCE IS
In Your Future

Six months from now, you'll look back on this book as one of the most incredible reads you've ever enjoyed, because the benefits you've gotten from all of the people you've influenced over these months wasn't possible until you read that book. I'll bet you already want to share your gratitude with the author, because you enjoyed it so much.

When you're influencing people, one of the best ways to persuade them is to build a future that includes your suggested outcomes.

Think about what you're doing next Saturday. There's already a picture a picture in your mind. Imagine what you'll be doing in one month, six months, a year. Your Unconscious has a notion of those things, too.

Your Unconscious mind is continually moving in the direction of a future that it has already devised inside your mind, so you want to build a new future for your subject to move towards.

To move people into a favorable trance, help them build that future event in their mind. Don't just take them to the event – take them beyond it, where your outcome is a certainty because it has already happened in their mind. In hypnosis, this is called Future Pacing.

For example, one of the ways I help people make the decision to attend my live workshops is:

> "Joe, imagine that you've attended my workshop and six months has passed since you graduated the course. You've spent several months using these techniques, seeing the results, hearing others praise you and feeling confident. Looking back on the training, what was the most important thing you got out of it?"

This language locks in the notion that they will come to my training and will get immense benefit from attending, all without actually telling him to come.

Here are some examples of using Future Pacing in everyday conversation:

> "Amy, how good will you feel a year from now, knowing that it was this security system that has been keeping your family safe, secure and worry-free?"

> "You're going to look back on this day as one of the most satisfying decisions you've ever made."

"In the future, when you think about how it used to be in the past, before you took this product home, you'll probably chuckle at how easy it is now, after all those years of struggle."

CHAPTER SEVEN

HYPNOTIC
Double Binds

When it comes to influencing others, it's important to remember that nobody likes to be manipulated against their will. People always want to feel as if they have choice.

Novice influencers are always trying to force their subjects to do something, which is why they only get results with those who are already easily manipulated. A hypnotic ninja takes no pride in manipulation. The ninja skills are more about creating win-win situations where people *want* to do what you're asking.

There's no coercion, no persuasion, no manipulation. The subject wants to make it happen.

When people feel as if they have no choice, they will resist your influence at nearly all cost. The way to keep people open to your suggestions is to always offer choice — even if it's only the illusion of choice. Enter the hypnotic double bind.

When my son was a young boy, his bedtime was 9:00 PM. Some nights — especially the nights where he was hyper — I would want him to go to bed early, so I would offer him a choice.

I would say:

> "Jonathan, I'm going to let you stay up to watch your favorite show on TV. You tell me, do you want to go to bed at 8:45 PM or at a quarter-to-nine when it's over?"

Of course, he would always say, enthusiastically, "Quarter to nine, dad!" Of course, to his young mind, a quarter-to-nine sounded later, even though they were both the actually the same time.

The purpose of the double bind is to give people the illusion of choice, so they feel comfortable having options, but both options actually result in the same exact outcome. In sales, this is often called the "Alternative Advance Close."

The trick is to think of what you want your subject to do, then come up with two ways for them to do it. Those two ways become your double bind.

For example, if I want someone to purchase my book, I might say:

> "Joe, which would you rather go home with today, the paperback or the hardback?" Notice, I'm not offering the prospect the choice of "No thanks, I'm not interested." The double bind is about choosing one or the other. In either case, both choices result in the same thing — a sale for me.

In my therapy office, I often ask the client, "Would you rather go into trance quickly, or a little more slowly?"

Double binds are to be used subtly and gently. If you're mowing people down with double binds left and right you're likely to get a reputation as a verbal bully, so use them with care, or you can just choose to be careful how you use them. It's totally up to you.

CHAPTER EIGHT

THE ART OF

The Never-Ending Quote

Quoting another source — especially a source of authority — is a highly hypnotic way of influencing a person.

People tend to be naturally influenced by those of high prestige and authority anyway. But when you're quoting a person who is not in the vicinity to defend themselves, it's very difficult to argue with them.

For instance, if I told you that I'm afraid of aliens coming in UFOs and tried to convince you that they'll pillage the world and kill all human beings, you might tell me that I'm completely nuts.

However, if I tell you that renowned quantum physicist Stephen Hawking, one of the most knowledgeable people on the subject of space, is certain of alien life and thinks we should fear them. He said, "I imagine they might exist in massive ships, having used up all the resources from their home planet. Such advanced aliens would perhaps become nomads, looking to conquer and colonise whatever planets they can reach." (By the way, that's a real quote)

Well, now, that becomes a little harder to argue with, now doesn't it?

Now, imagine if I said to you, "The other day, I was talking to my brother-in-law, who's boss told him the most interesting thing that he read in an article in TIME Magazine, where Stephen Hawking said..."

At this point, two things happen. First, it becomes virtually impossible to argue against the point. The listener just ends up accepting the final premise. Second, it becomes so hard for the listener to keep track of who said what to whom, that they actually produce a mild trance and become *even more* influenceable.

The other day, I was talking to this woman, Susan, who's husband came to one of my NLP trainings, and he told her about this guy Greg in the class who was getting instructions from another student who told him that this is one of the easiest ways to get people to accept a suggestion.

Of course, as with most things, there is a point of diminishing returns. You can only extend the quote out to about eight to twelve people before your listener will get confused, get annoyed and tune out. So pay attention, and, as with all hypnotic ninja techniques, use it subtly.

CHAPTER NINE

BEING

Artfully Vague

As you think about all those ways that you know how to communicate, you know that, often, one has that certain ability. That realization you have, right as you hear one certain thing or another, is better, isn't it? Because you know that they know how hypnotic artful vagueness is when they do it right.

Did the above paragraph make your head spin a little? You may have noticed that, while there are a lot of words, it really didn't say much at all. That's because it is "artfully vague."

Renowned hypnotherapist, Milton H. Erickson, was well known for this kind of hypnotic speech, because he created a hypnotic style based on it.

Imagine that inside your mind is a search engine, just like the one you would use on the internet. If I say "moon," your mind does a quick lookup, and one result comes up - the moon.

But if I say "flower," your unconscious has to do a little more work. There are more things that are "flower," than just one.

However, even this is a quick search, because you'll likely come up with a picture or memory of your favorite flower as your first result.

Now, if I say, "All those thoughts you were thinking yesterday... yes, *those* thoughts," things get even tougher. That's not even something your conscious mind can hold in your awareness, which is limited in capacity, compared to your unconscious mind.

Your unconscious mind has to do the search and then shuffle through thousands of results, trying to find out which meaning to deliver to your conscious mind as a thought.

During this search process, which Milton used to call a *transderivational search,* you are in trance, and your conscious mind's ability to reason, analyze, think logically and — most importantly — reject suggestions, is greatly diminished.

The rule is very simple: Concrete concepts can be accepted or rejected by the conscious mind on their face value. Abstract or vague concepts *must* be contemplated to even be understood.

There are several ways that you can use ambiguous speech, which we call *ambiguities*, to keep a person in a light trance and make them more persuadable.

Universal Statements

A universal statement is anything you say that includes either everything or nothing. For example, if I say "Thinking of all your thoughts," it's universal because of the word, "all." In other words, it's not referring to a specific thought, which makes the mind go into trance to find a thought.

This sentence is loaded with universals, "Using universals always produces trance in every situation, all the time, and never does nothing."

The following words are universal in nature: all, none, everything, nothing, always, never, everybody, nobody, total, complete.

Frozen Actions

Frozen actions happen when you turn a verb (action word) into a noun (person, place or thing word). For example, if I say, "We have to keep communication here," it sounds as if "communication," is a thing — but it's not!

"Communication involves the act of "communicating," which involves many styles, many steps, and happens over time. By turning it into a "thing," we confuse the mind, because it can't actually make a picture of it, and pictures are one of the primary ways in which the mind thinks.

The way to test if a word is a Frozen Action is by asking yourself, "Can I put this in a wheelbarrow?"

If you've ever been to a conference, filled with corporate buzz-words (which are almost always Frozen Actions), you know how mind-numbing these can be. Your mind starts to wander off to a distant place, because the words you're hearing should have meaning, but it's too hard to figure out. Your conscious mind finally surrenders, and trance occurs.

The following words are Frozen Verbs which can produce a light trance: thoughts, feelings, emotions, cares, worries, fears, hesitation, anticipation, enjoyment, fulfillment.

Often, you can turn an action word into a Frozen Action by adding the letter "-s," the letters "-tion," or the letters "-ment" to the end of the verb.

Ambiguous Actions

Ambiguous actions are action words that don't tell you how to do the action. If I tell you to reject the politics of the world, what does that mean? Does that mean to dislike them, hate them, protest against them, or something else?

There's no information in the word that tells you how to do it, so the unconscious mind has to go inside, search the search engine, and try to come up with an action that matches.

These words can be very hypnotic when used properly. Here are a few Ambiguous Action words: try, do, fiddle, subdue, communicate, maneuver, manipulate, control.

Ambiguous Subjects

If you remember back to elementary school grammar, every sentence is supposed to have a *subject* — a word with specifies the person, place or thing you're talking about.

Of course, we hypnotic ninjas forget to specify things when

we're being ambiguous. Using the Ambiguous Subject means that you leave out or confuse whom you're referring to.

For example, if I say, "They really like to use hypnotic language," who am I talking about? The word "they," is ambiguous.

People can use this language pattern (which people?). Because they are very good (they, meaning the people, or they, meaning the language patterns?). When one masters this pattern (one who?), the people will be influenced (which ones?).

Some Ambiguous Subject words are: they, them, it, those, people, one, many, some, anybody,

One-Sided Comparisons

One-Sided Comparisons are more confusing. They tend to work better. It's because they're more ambiguous. They have a greater capacity for trance, because they're quicker.

You may notice in the four sentences above, that something important is left out. In each sentence, there's a comparison being made — more, better, more, greater, quicker. But what am I comparing to?

In each of the sentences, the comparing item is left out, so the comparison is one-sided. This does two things. First, it causes the person to go "inside" to try to figure out what the comparison is. Second, it makes the suggestion *easier* to accept (did you catch that?).

For example, if I said to you, "You should buy this new car. It's more affordable than an apple," you would laugh me off the lot! The comparison is obviously bogus!

But, if I instead said, "You should buy this new car. It's definitely more affordable," then my suggestion that the car is affordable is more easily accepted.

This is a highly hypnotic method of communication, but remember, it's *better* to leave the comparison one-sided.

One-sided comparison words are: better, worse, more, less, easier, harder, brighter, dimmer, heavier, lighter, cheaper, pricier.

You can use virtually any normal comparison word, just remember to leave off the thing you're comparing to.

CHAPTER TEN

HYPNOTIC STORIES
And Metaphors

By far, the most hypnotic form of influence is metaphor. Metaphors are hypnotic stories that lead a person into the trance you desire for them.

I once trained a student named Todd who, after learning some of my hypnotic language patterns went home to Arizona.

He tried explaining this and that to his wife, about all the thing he had learned, but she simply wasn't getting it. He said, "Honey, if you *learn to use these patterns*, everything is possible. A person can have anything they want. They can have love, happiness, contentment, profit... anything at all."

Of course, she was skeptical. His wife had been telling her best friend about all the things that Todd had told her that I said about hypnotic influence being the most effective ways of communicating.

He said, "Really honey, this way of communicating is better and I can prove it! All you have to do is *use it*. Just try one little language pattern each day, and they'll start to *become habit*."

She said, "Fine, you can make me *believe this hypnosis stuff works*, by overcoming a challenge. If I find that *it's better than normal language,* I'll believe you and I'll start to *use it everyday."*

That day, they were walking along the street, admiring the nature on their walk. They could see the colors of nature dancing in the lazy wind. They could hear the melodic tweeting of the birds and feel the warm sun beating down on their faces.

So she challenged him. She said, "When we get to the coffee shop, you work your magic, and if you can get a cup of coffee for free, I'll *be convinced."*

At the coffee shop, after taking his wife's order, he began having a conversation with the barrista by meeting her in her trance.

He said, "It seems like you're working hard."

She replied, "Yeah! But I like my job."

He said, "That's better, isn't it? To have that special thing that you love. That makes it the most enjoyable thing in the world, but I'll bet it's not as enjoyable as that vacation you went on."

She lit up said, "No! How did you know about that?"

He continued, "Isn't it nice to know that as you think about that now, the memory of it makes you feel wonderful? It kind of breaks you out of your work and makes you feel better, doesn't it? It's nice when you can *give someone a gift* like that, isn't it? *Like me,* I really do love to go on vacation. Where I can *be free* to just do something that makes me feel good, because *you want to,* ya know?"

At that point, she smiled, blushed a little and cocked her head and said, "Hey, would you like a cup of coffee while you're waiting? It's on the house."

As you look back over that story, you may notice several things, but first, I'll tell you my intention for the story.

Of course, the overt purpose of the story is to tell you something interesting, or entertaining. My covert purpose was to "install" in you the idea to practice this everyday, and the belief that hypnotic influence works.

This is, by the way, a true story from one of my graduates, Todd in Arizona.

Hypnotic metaphors don't have to be true, but telling true stories helps to keep track of the details. Plus, the stories that are personal to you are the one's you'll be able to associate to ("get into") the most.

Of course, the story contains many of the hypnotic influence patterns that you've learned, throughout this book. There was also extended use of quotes to help you accept my suggestions that are built into the story.

There's one other great tidbit in these stories, called "Embedded Commands." These are words which are somehow distinguished from the other words of the story. In writing, they're often italicized, bolded or underlined. In speaking, they're often said with a lower tone of voice, or a slower speed.

Your unconscious mind is very good at picking up on these differences, but you conscious mind usually misses them. So, the suggestions go directly into the unconscious.

Go back over the story and look for them. They're there!

These suggestions can be embedded in almost any communication — even if it has nothing to do with the command!

The founders of NLP used to tell a story that started with, "Remember when Mom used to bake cookies from *scratch*? *Your* mom used to do that, right? Everybody *knows* what that's like," and within minutes, the whole audience was scratching and rubbing their nose, because the command "scratch your nose (knows)" was subtly emphasized in the sentence!

Practice these embedded commands and get to the point where you can speak them in a lower tone of voice or slower speed, subtly, so the conscious mind doesn't catch on. Your suggestions will go directly into the unconscious mind.

PART TWO

Hypnotic Language Reference

PATTERN ONE
Mind Reading

Claiming to know the thoughts or feelings of another person without saying how you knew, as if you were reading their mind.

Examples:

I know that you're excited about Milton Model patterns...

I know you're wondering. . .

I know you believe. . . .

I know you came here for a purpose.

I know how you like that.

I know you enjoy. . .

I know that you knew that.

I know you're thinking how wonderful trance is.

I know that you're in a nice trance now.

I know that you're learning a lot here today.

I know that tomorrow you will learn even more than today.

I know that when you leave this training, you will be much wiser.

I know you all studied very hard before you came here.

We know you don't care.

I knew you were thinking that.

I'm sure you're aware. . .

I'm sure you felt. . .

You probably are aware. . .

You probably also know

I bet you're upset about that.

I realize you already know. . .

I can tell you're happy.

I can tell how you feel. . .

I can tell you've had a trying day.

I can see you believe. . .

I see that you know. . .

You are enjoying this book, now, aren't you?

PATTERN TWO
Lost Performative

Sharing a value judgment on someone or something, but not saying who is did the judging.

Examples:

It's good to know that a person can think such things...

It's bad to…

That's good.

That's right.

That's too bad.

It's good when…

That's perfect!

It is important to…

It's wrong to cheat.

One doesn't have to…

Today is a great day!

It's best to do therapy.

It's good to study hard.

It's important to learn.

It's good to dispute that

No one should judge others.

It's great to always be right!

It's great that you can change.

It's really good that you say that.

It's better to give than to receive.

It was not right of you to say that.

You're wrong. (Or: "That's right... you're wrong.)

And it's a good thing to wonder (Nominalization: "thing")

You shouldn't be judging the comments of other people.

PATTERN THREE
Cause and Effect

Implying that one thing causes or caused another. It's not necessary for it to be true, only to sound plausible.

Implied Causatives include:

a. "Because, when you think them, you'll find yourself intranced."

b. "Makes"

c. "If..., then..."

d. "As you... then you..."

e. "Since…"

f. Any C>E relationship, regardless of the language used to imply it.

Examples:

If I help you, then you'll learn this.

As you sit there, then you can feel

Don't X, unless you want to Y.

Don't sit there unless you want to go into trance.

Don't move your foot unless you want to go deeper.

If you sit in this chair, you'll go into trance.

As you listen closely, you will learn faster.

As you sit there you can feel more confident.

Reading this sentence, you get better and better.

You can hear the music helping you to relax now

Just your being here makes you want to learn this.

As you ask that question, then you begin to understand.

Because we are here, you are learning many new things

As you sit here and listen to this, you are learning so much.

Because you are here you are going to learn NLP more easily.

You will become more relaxed as you feel the fresh air coming in.

As you contemplate Milton Model, you can go deeply into trance.

. . . .And that's because it's artfully vague.

PATTERN FOUR
Complex Equivalence

Referring to two things as being equal, as in their meanings being equivalent.

"And that means you can think even more."

"To be," is, am, are, equals

Examples:

You are relaxing, which means you're going into trance.

When you get moved, you'll be happy.

Being here means that you will change.

Your question means you know it already.

Asking questions means you are learning.

Going to bed early means you will be alert.

Your body relaxing means you're becoming more comfortable.

You know the answer, which means you are competent.

Regular exercise means you are a better athlete.

Your being in this group means your trance will deepen.

Being here means you will enjoy the process.

Breathing that way means you'll go even deeper

Sitting in this room is an indication that you are learning

many things.

Your relaxed body means that you are in trance now.

The fact that you want to learn, means that you will.

Just getting here means that you're willing to change.

Mastering these skills means you're a better therapist.

You're learning many things because he is a good teacher.

As you exercise regularly, it means you will get healthy.

Keeping your eyes open like that means you'll go into trance.

And closing your eyes means you'll go even deeper. (Double bind)

You've come a long way, and that means that you're ready to change.

You're listening closely means you're learning wonderful things.

Your trance-ability means you'll change your behavior.

PATTERN FIVE

Presuppositions

Any language which presupposes or assumes a statement or an outcome.

Examples:

And those thoughts you're thinking...

You can do this even better.

You're learning many things.

You are changing all the time.

How else do you go into trance?

You can see this more clearly now.

You're seeing things differently now.

You'll be able to learn even more tomorrow.

You are going to go into a deeper trance soon.

After you pass this class, the next one is easier.

You can go through this process even more easily

You realize you have more resources than ever before.

Since your unconscious mind is listening all the time

You can easily move in the direction of your past memories.

How many ways do you know that you're unlimited?

There are five reasons you want to do this, the least of

which is that it's good for you.

Have you heard about the great results this product will get for you?

Don't think of a blue tree.

You can do this easily and effortlessly.

PATTERN SIX
Universal Quantifiers

Universal generalizations that don't specify who or what you're referring to.

Examples:

And all the thoughts… every one of them...

Nobody's perfect.

Everything you know

All the things to learn

All the people, all the time

Everything you have learned

So every time you think of that

all the feelings there are to feel

after all you have learned from the audios

with everything that's happening in the world

Everything is wonderful.

We are all in trance now.

Everything means nothing.

There is always tomorrow.

Everyone knows it to be true.

There is always more to learn.

All the meanings will be clear

Everybody knows this part is easy.

Everyone here has something to learn.

One can never know all there is to know.

Everybody knows you can learn all things.

Everything in this room enhances your learning.

Everyone can learn everything we're doing here today.

All the people doing this process are learning many new things

PATTERN SEVEN
Modal Operators

Words of possibility or necessity. These words usually form the rules in life (can/can't, should/shouldn't, must/mustn't, will/won't, etc.)

Examples:

Should let you know that you can.

You should care for others.

You should now clearly see

You should not hurry into trance just yet.

You shouldn't go into trance too quickly, now.

You should know it's OK to learn in this room.

You could learn this now.

You could write this down. . . . or not.

You could feel more and more peaceful.

You must be aware....

You must be getting this now. . .at some level. . . .

You may discover you can learn here.

You can change overnight.

You may hear the words of wisdom.

You can begin to get that change now.

And you can trust your unconscious mind.

You might be able to learn this quite easily.

It's possible to learn everything easily and quickly.

PATTERN EIGHT
Nominalizations

Verbs or processes that have been frozen in time by turning them into nouns. The test is, "Can I put it in a wheelbarrow?"

Examples

Because, those thoughts and patterns have a way touching your emotions.

(With minimal restructuring, I have taken various Nominalizations and linked them together for your reading enjoyment. Every (yes every) line contains a nominalization.)

NLP is easy

as you just trust in the process

while you're in trance

and allow your intuitions

to help you notice new feelings

as those feelings come

and other feelings may go

your behavior improves

so the renewed communication

in your relationships

means you have made many new learnings.

Because that communication

shows respect

for those relationships

and all your new decisions

showed your trust

in the importance of

your unconscious mind's

remarkably powerful desires

and your demonstration

of those new learnings

and understandings

showed your sense of wonder

at the importance

of all the work you've been doing

in your life

which is a perfect demonstration

of the simple truth

that trance works

doesn't it?

(By the way, did you notice that "nominalization" is a nominalization?)

PATTERN NINE
Unspecified Verbs

Verbs that don't specify the action taken. In other words, "what to do," is left out or left ambiguous.

Examples:

And you can use them easily…

I was wondering

if you knew

when you are feeling like you could

just let go

and notice how easily

you begin to enjoy

and as you continue

breathing

you may

or you may not

notice going deeper

and you could go deeper

since you really enjoy

doing this

and you could even continue

or if you don't

you may discover

how much you remember

about how you're improving, now

and you will, of course

be wondering

just where this might be going

so remember

if you will

that your being

and your learning

can only help

you to move

towards understanding

just how easily you can

be changing

and inducing

or simply t r a n c i n g o u t

aren't you?

PATTERN TEN

Tag Question

A question added after a statement, designed to displace resistance.

Example:

You're enjoying this, aren't you?

didn't I?

isn't it?

have you?

will you?

won't you?

haven't you?

aren't we?

aren't you?

don't you now?

don't you think?

won't you, now?

couldn't you . . .?

wouldn't you know?

and you can, can you not?

PATTERN ELEVEN
Lack of Referential Index

A phrase where the subject of the sentence is not a specific person or thing.

These are often used in advertisements and commercials.

Examples:

People do all the time...

People can

It is, you see.

That's the way.

People can learn

Now you've got it!

You will, you know.

One can easily see

You know the feeling.

You may not know it

You have, and you know it.

You can just let it go now.

A person can, you know....

That would help you go deeper.

It puts people through changes.

Do you see this more clearly, now?

One can, you know, accomplish a goal.

When you can notice that certain sensation right there

PATTERN TWELVE
Comparative Deletions

Comparison to someone or something that's not specified.

Because the second item cannot be represented in the mind (it is missing), the unconscious mind has to assume the comparison to be true.

Examples:

And I think that you know it's better that way...

Right or wrong....

even more relaxed

It's a higher thought

You will enjoy it more.

You're doing better now

Now and then, things happen

But that's neither here not there.

You're going deeper and deeper....

Sooner or later you will understand.

This is more or less the right time

before or after you come out of trance.

At one time or another, you may notice

and it's more or less the right thing to do

But it's better to change now. (Also: Lost Performative)

And it's better to do it that way. (Also: Lost Performative)

You're a better person than you were before. (Did you notice both?)

PATTERN THIRTEEN
Pacing Current Experience

Describing the client's experience in a way which is undeniable.

Examples:

You are sitting here, listening to the sound of my voice and thinking those thoughts and that means…

You hear my voice

We are in this group

As we sit here now. . . .

And you're sitting here

As you notice each blink

As you continue breathing. . . .

As you look at me like that. . . .

And as you breathe in. . . . and out

As you kneel there sipping your tea,

As you feel the weight of the notebook on your lap. . . .

As you're looking around

More of your muscles are relaxing.

As you stop and look and listen

You can feel the warmth of the cup on your lips. . . .

While you are sitting there writing. . . .

As you hear that plane overhead. . . .

As your eyes continue reading the words on this page while you're looking at it and from time to time you may become aware of the thoughts in your mind or those sensations in your hand or down there on the soles of your feet you could also begin to wonder if you could think of how artfully you can pace a person's ongoing experience.

PATTERN FOURTEEN
Double Bind

Offering the illusion of choice to make sure the client does what you want them to, because both choices are the same.

Examples:

You can either choose to change immediately, or let it happen automatically now.

Do you want to begin now, or later?

As you dream, or upon awakening. . . .

either before, or after, leaving this room

When you go to bed you will either dream, or not.

Will you begin to change now or after this session?

Would you like to quit smoking today or tomorrow?

Would you like to buy the car now, or test drive it first?

Would you rather do that before or after your meeting?

You either will or you won't   [followed by an unspecified verb]

Would you like to go to bed at 8:45, or at a quarter till nine?

Do you want to learn that today or during your next session?

Take all the time you need to finish up in the next five minutes.

You can change as quickly or as slowly as you want to now.

PATTERN FIFTEEN
Conversational Postulate

A permissive command that sounds like a question. Always delivered with a downturn of the tone of the voice at the end.

Examples:

Would you be happy to do that now?

Can you imagine this?

Can you close the door?

Will you just let go now?

Can you picture doing this?

Can you see what I'm saying?

Can you reach that level now?

Would it be all right to feel this good?

Do you know that you know it already?

Could you open your mind for a moment?

How easily do you think you can do this?

Can you remember to be kind to yourself?

Does this sound like it will work for you?

Do you feel prepared to sign the contract now?

Do you think you can make the changes you want?

Would you like. . . to just sit here. . . and relax now?

Wouldn't you like to just drift into that peaceful state?

Is this something you could see yourself buying now?

PATTERN SIXTEEN
Extended Quotes

Quoting a person, who quotes another, who quotes another, etc, becoming impossible to tell where one quote leaves off and the next begins.

Examples:

Last week I was with Andrew who told me about when he attended Practitioner Training in 2008, when he talked to Tim who said that his mother learned from a TV show that NLP is life-changing.

Last year, in San Diego, John Grinder was telling us about this African drummer who asked Judy if she had heard the village chief say how easy it is to generate extended quotes.
Last year, I met a woman who said she knew a man
who had mentioned
that his Father told him. . . .
Michael said that in a training four years ago,
he had told the story about when
Richard Bandler was quoting
Virginia Satir, who used to say that. . .
I was speaking with a friend the other day, who told me

of a

conversation she had had with a therapist who told her about a session he'd had with a client who said. . . .

When I went to Laguna the other day with Van and Carlo, one of them told a story about when his mother would sit down and explain to the children how Father had said. . .

The other day, a participant in the training was telling me that her husband said Michael had told him to ask you to think of a couple of extended quotes yourself.

PATTERN SEVENTEEN

Selectional Restriction Violation

Personifying an inanimate thing. For example, a body part. This is the construction of many metaphors.

Example:

That TV was pretty smart…

My rock said. . . .

The walls have ears

That nail hurt my tire.

Flowers like to be picked.

My car knows how to get here.

Put the noise down in your toe, and let it listen.

What did your actions say to you?

Could you open your mind for a moment?

and just listen to what the butterfly has to tell you?

because the words have power of their own

The cat doesn't care about the furniture's outrage from the scratching.

As he picked up the spoon, the Jell-O trembled with fear.

And if your pen told us all the things it has learned....

My car loves to go fast when the road beckons.

Do trees cry when they drop their leaves?

Sometime the cookies just call to you.

Do you know what the pen thought?

These wall can tell such stories.

PATTERN EIGHTEEN
Phonological Ambiguities

Words with different meanings that sound alike.

Examples:

So, as you hear those things when you here is a safe place to learn…

"Hear," "Here"

"There," "They're," "Their"

"Son," "Sun"

PATTERN NINETEEN
Syntactic Ambiguities

Words with ambiguous syntax – where you can't tell what part of the sentence a word applies to.

Examples:

You realize how hypnotizing hypnotists can be tricky.

"They are visiting relatives"

"Speaking to you as a child..."

PATTERN TWENTY
Scope Ambiguity

Words with ambiguous scope – where you can't tell how much of the sentence a word applies to.

Examples:

"And those good thoughts and feelings bring even more…"

"The old men & women..."

"The disturbing noises & thoughts..."

"The weight of your hands & feet..."

PATTERN TWENTY-ONE

Punctuation

Using punctuation ambiguously to implant suggestions or direct thoughts.

There are several ways you can do this:

Run on sentences:

"So as you continue to pay attention to the only thing that you can <u>pay attention to… me</u>, I think this is fascinating."

The embedded command is, "pay attention to me."

"I wonder if you can notice your <u>hand me the glass</u>."

The embedded command is "hand me the glass," and pivots on the word "hand."

Pausing at improper places:

"I wonder how well you'll <u>close your eyes and sleep</u> (pause) peacefully tonight."

"Perhaps you'll find it easy to go <u>deeper</u> (pause) into the reasons why you want to succeed."

The embedded command is to "go deeper" (presumably, into trance).

Incomplete sentences, where the sentence is left unfinished (forced mind-reads):

"Because I know you'd like to go into a nice, deep… that's right."

"You know you should buy right now, because there's no better time than the…"

Remember, anything you can get the client to say will be more powerful than you saying it yourself.

PATTERN TWENTY-TWO

Utilization

Using what the other person has said, done or related from their model of the world so as to keep rapport and develop trance.

Client says, "You're not going to hypnotize me."

You say, "That's right I'm not going to hypnotize you, because the only person who can close your eyes, relax and go deep inside, is you."

Client says, "I'm not sold."

You say, "That's right, you're not sold, yet, because you haven't asked the one question that will have you totally and completely sold, right now."

PART THREE

Creating Metaphors

That Work

CREATING

Metaphors

Metaphors use the language of the mind (symbols) and hypnotic language to create powerful "healing stories" that help your clients to resolve problems at the unconscious level – often even without their conscious awareness.

Creating a metaphor consists of four basic steps:

1. Create characters or objects in the story that correspond to the people and relationships in the actual situation.

2. Pace the client's problem by having those characters and objects behave in a similar way to the current situation.

3. Giving the main character in the story some internal resource (state, strategy or new behavior) that the client is missing in the current situation.

4. Finish the story by having the character resolve the conflict and achieve their outcome.

The following two pages will show how to create a metaphor using these steps.

METAPHORS
Pre-Mapping Strategies

1. Clearly identify the problem

   Do not proceed until you know the problem is a problem. Ask, "How is that a problem?"

2. Analyze their strategy

   Does the client have an unresourceful strategy? If so, you can install a new strategy through the metaphor. This is the basic principle behind stories like The Little Engine that Could

3. Identify new outcomes, choices and solutions

   It's important to always have an outcome or solution in mind. You can state it specifically or ambiguously, but you should avoid unconscious connection.

   Ask, "What is this an example of?" Then, "What are other examples of this?" to get possible resolutions.

4. Create anchors for strategic elements in the solution

   For example, you might anchor all the resources from the main character on the knee.

METAPHORS
Mapping Strategies

1.   Create Related Characters, Places and Objects. Map over all the nouns (persons, places, things) of importance to create the elements of the story. Be creative, and allow your imagination to run free. Characters can be anything animate or inanimate. What you choose is not nearly as important as preserving the relationships between the characters. You can use well-known characters, like those from fairy tales or nursery rhymes.

2.   Create Related Processes and Behaviors. Map over all verbs of importance to create the action of the story, including behaviors and strategies used by the client, if known, pacing the clients current situation.

3.   Generate New Resources for the Client. You can do this through reframing, reaccessing forgotten resources, installing a new strategy and more. The metaphor should presuppose that the client is at cause for the problem and the solution. You may choose to keep the specifics of the resource ambiguous, to let your client come to some of their own conclusions and solutions.

4.   Use Non-Sequiturs, Ambiguous Language and Direct Quotes.
If the client's conscious mind is getting in the way of the effect of the metaphor, use linguistic confusion techniques

to distract the conscious mind. Conscious awareness of the purpose of the metaphor does not necessarily interfere with the process, but it is likely that it will.

5.   Keep the Resolution as Ambiguous as Necessary. The metaphor is for your client's unconscious mind – not their conscious mind. So keep the resolution at the unconscious level by keeping it ambiguous. Allow the unconscious to figure out the exact steps based on the metaphor you give them. If possible, future pace the story to lock in and test the results.

METAPHORS

Making Metaphors Work

Steps for constructing and delivering metaphors:

1. Ask questions to get the Present State

2. Ask questions to get the Desired State

3. Ask questions about the problem such as, "What Prevents You?"

4. Ask about what is of Interest or value to the client. "What's Important to you?"

5. Ask yourself, "What is this an example of? What are other examples of this?"

6. Create the metaphor: Bridge the Gap to New Resources

PART FOUR

Final Words From

Your Sensei

GO FORTH AND
Be Influential,
Grasshopper

Throughout this book, you're seeing new ways to speak to people. Ways of communicating that influence others like never before. As you watch the results you get from these techniques unfold, you'll find yourself becoming a hypnotic influence ninja.

You've been reading this book, page by page, chapter by chapter, learning many new things, and that means *you're growing*. I'm not going to suggest that this will be your favorite hypnosis book of all time, but as you finish this book in its entirety, you're becoming more confident, more effective and more charismatic.

After you visit my web page at www.LearnHypnosisNow. com and discover all of the ways you'll learn to become a SUPER hypnotic influence ninja, you'll be practically unstoppable. It's your desire to *take my online courses* or live classes that will make you even more successful, or perhaps just that much more happy.

Ultimately, the best way to be persuasive is to always influence with integrity, speak from your heart, and seek win-win outcomes for everyone involved.

Years from now, when you're still getting results from learning this, perhaps you'll look back on it as a fond memory, or maybe you'll just really enjoy it. Either way, I know that the many friends you've recommended this book to will love you for it, now, don't they?

Go now, ninja. Your destiny awaits!

SPECIAL OFFER

YOU KNOW IT'S

Time For A Change

Y ou've been reading this book, and seeing the wonderful ways in which being more influential can improve your life. You know you've just scratched the surface, and that means that there's so much more to learn about making your life magnificent.

Imagine what it would be like to have happiness, wealth, love, health, and more *in abundance*. What would it be like to see yourself having all you want in life as a result of having learned from me?

As you read these pages and wonder what else there is, I invite you to check out my new event, The Power to Create Your Life... Now! This three day event will change your life for the better, forever. But don't take my word for it, visit www.transformdestiny.com/create-your-life to find out the truth about what you're capable of.

It's normally $797 for General Admission, but use the following coupon at checkout and get your General Admission ticket for Just $97, Preferred ticket for just $197 or Premier ticket for just $247!

Coupon Code: Ninja

ABOUT THE AUTHOR

MASTER HYPNOTIST

Michael Stevenson

Michael Stevenson is a Master Hypnotherapist and Trainer of Hypnosis and Neuro-Linguistic Programming.

He's the author of the best-selling book, Learn Hypnosis... Now! the easiest book to read to learn how to hypnotize yourself and others.

Michael is the owner of Transform Destiny, a transformation and training center in Orange County, California where you can take live trainings in NLP, Hypnosis, TIME Techniques, EFT Success Coaching, Personal Development and more.

Michael's current masterpiece is The Power to Create Your Life... Now! (www.tdnlp.com/cyl), a weekend course that will change your life forever.

You can reach Michael and read about his online courses and live trainings and workshops at www.transformdestiny.com.

Made in the USA
Charleston, SC
08 January 2013